MONTVALE PUBLIC LIBRARY, NJ

3 9125 05028993 3

S0-FLO-857

ON LINE

MONTVALE PUBLIC LIBRARY

J 78200
629.47 Greene, Carol
GRE   At the space
        center

DEMCO

At the Space Center

Design and Art Direction

Lindaanne Donohoe Design

Illustrations

Penny Dann

Picture Credits

All photographs courtesy of NASA,

The National Aeronautics and Space Administration

• • • • • • • • • • • • • •

Library of Congress Cataloging-in-Publication Data

Greene, Carol.

At the space center / by Carol Greene.

p.   cm.

Summary: A simple overview of the operations at several
space flight centers in the United States.

ISBN 1-56766-484-9 (reinforced Lib. bdg.)

1. Launch complexes (Astronautics)—United States—Juvenile literature.

[1. Launch complexes (Astronautics) 2. Space flight.]   I. Title.

TL4026.G74   1998   97-41837

629.47'8—dc21   CIP

AC

Copyright 1998 by The Child's World®, Inc.
All rights reserved. No part of this book may be reproduced or utilized
without written permission from the publisher.

At the Space Center

By Carol Greene

The Child's World®, Inc.

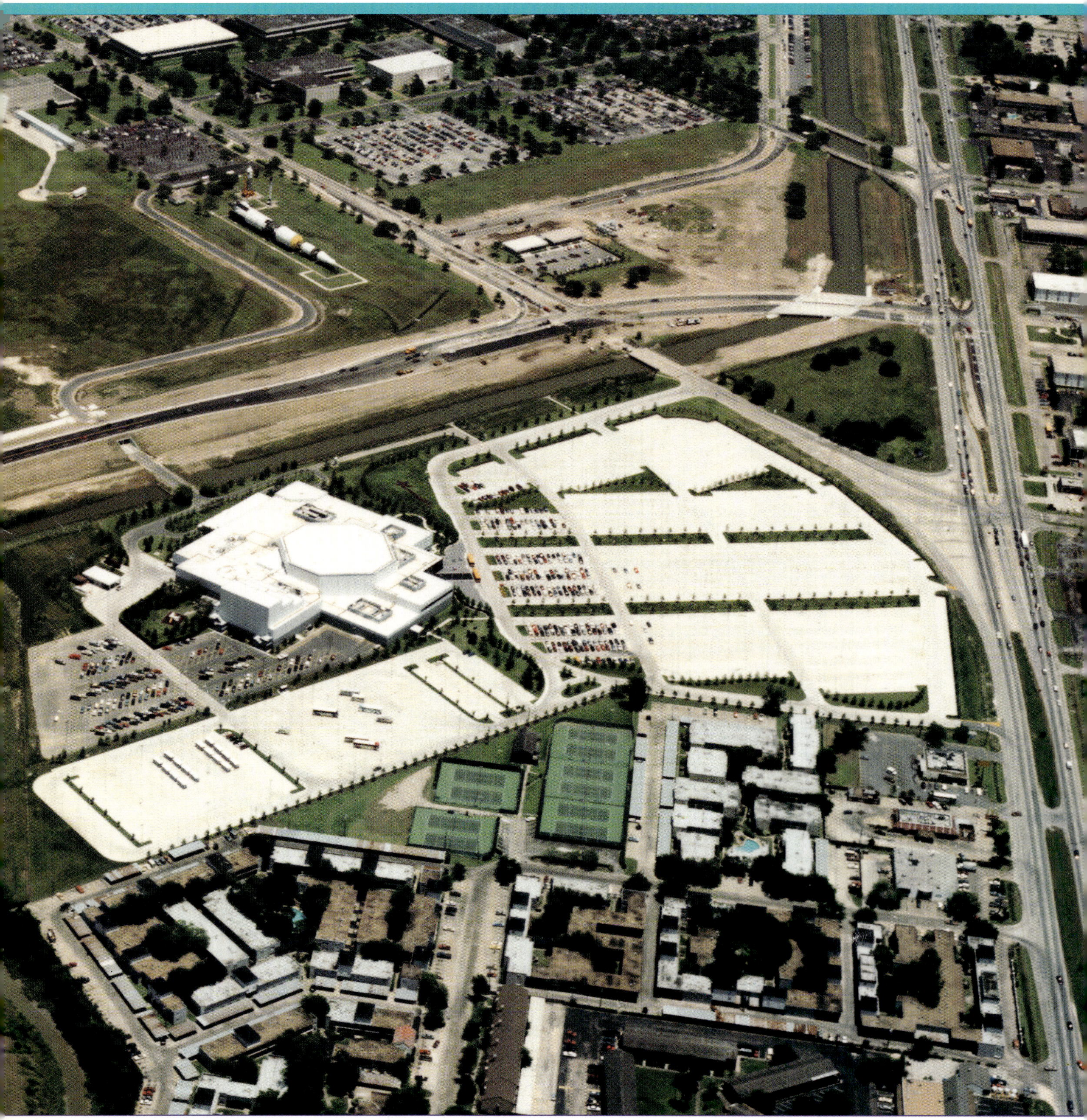

There are several space centers in the United States. They are all run by NASA—the National Aeronautics and Space Administration. NASA is part of the U.S. government. Let's start at the Lyndon B. Johnson Space Center in Houston, Texas.

Here we are in Houston, Texas.

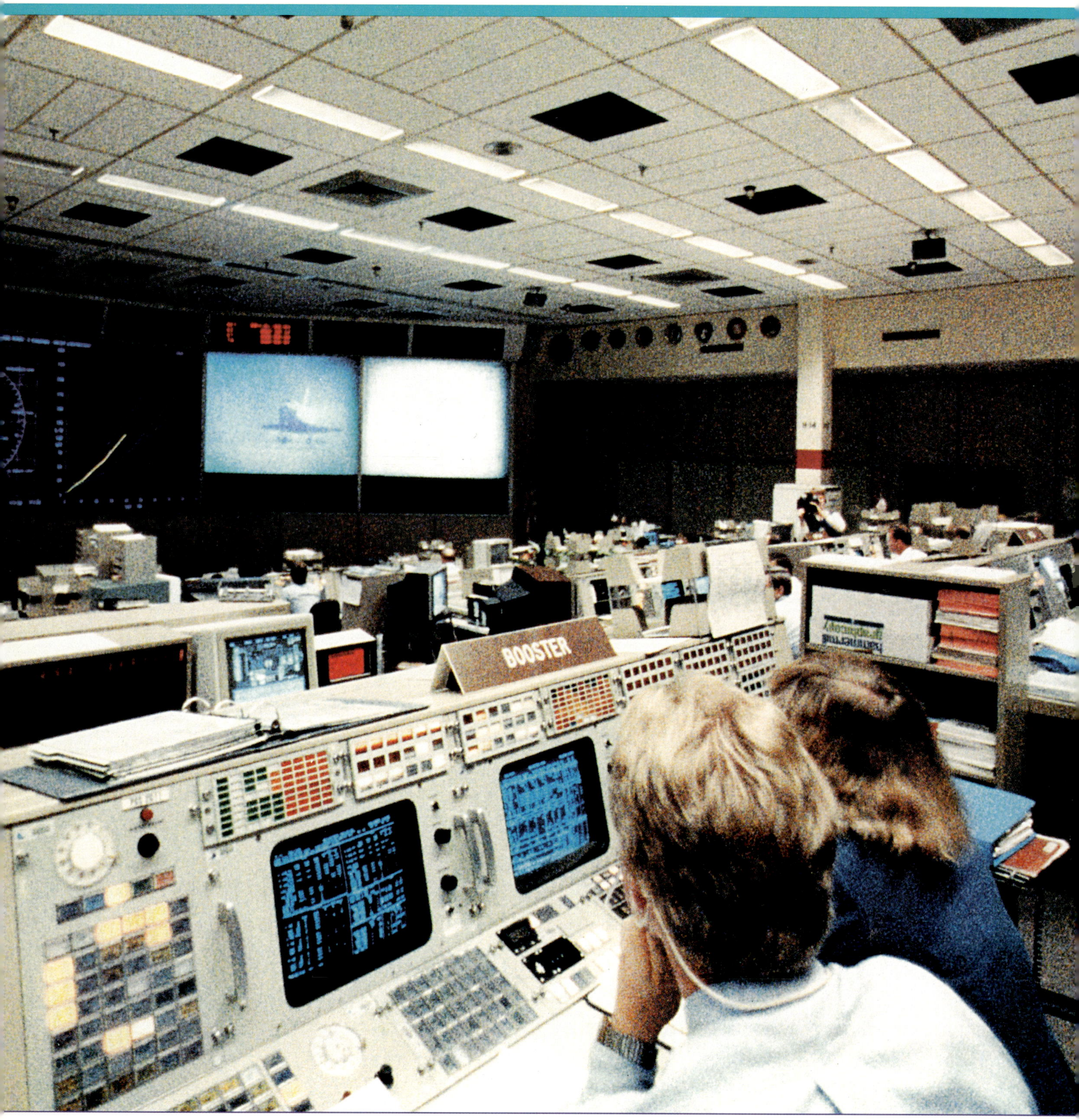
BOOSTER

Mission Control is at the Johnson Space Center. These people work with the astronauts who are out in space. *YAKITY! YAK!*

The people at Mission Control keep spacecraft flying safely. They talk to the astronauts by radio, too.

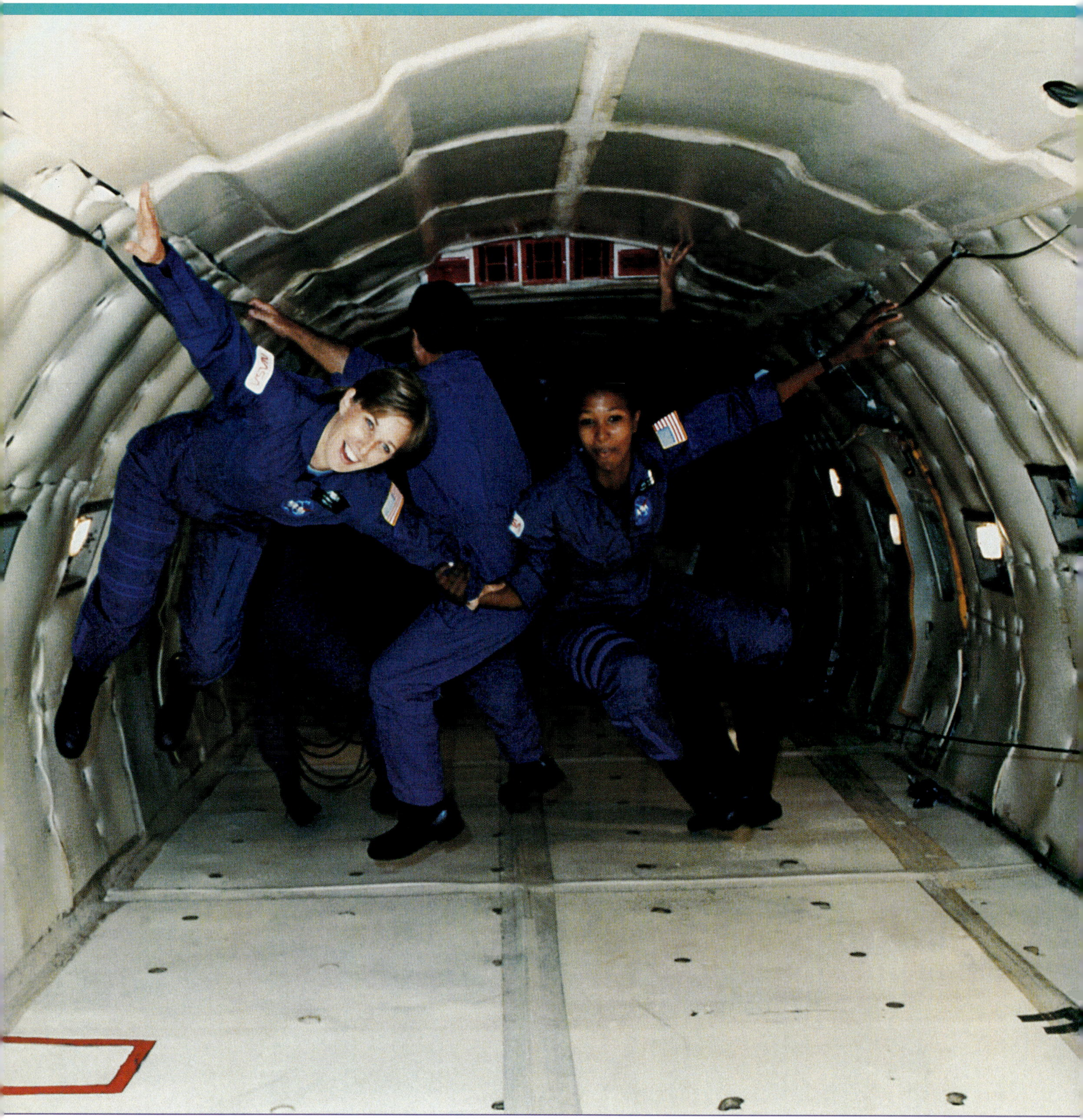

Astronauts get all their training at Johnson Space Center. These astronauts are flying in a special plane. It shows them how it feels to be weightless— to weigh nothing. WHEEE!

Sometimes astronauts call this plane "the Vomit Comet."

UnitedStates
SPACE SHUTTLE ORBITER
REMOTE MANIPULATOR
SYSTEM
SPACE
SHUTTLE
MISSION
PROFILE

At Space Center Houston, visitors learn all about Johnson Space Center. Here you can watch films, look at spacecraft, and listen to Mission Control. You can even touch a rock from the moon.

WOW! Engineers plan new spacecraft at Johnson Space Center.

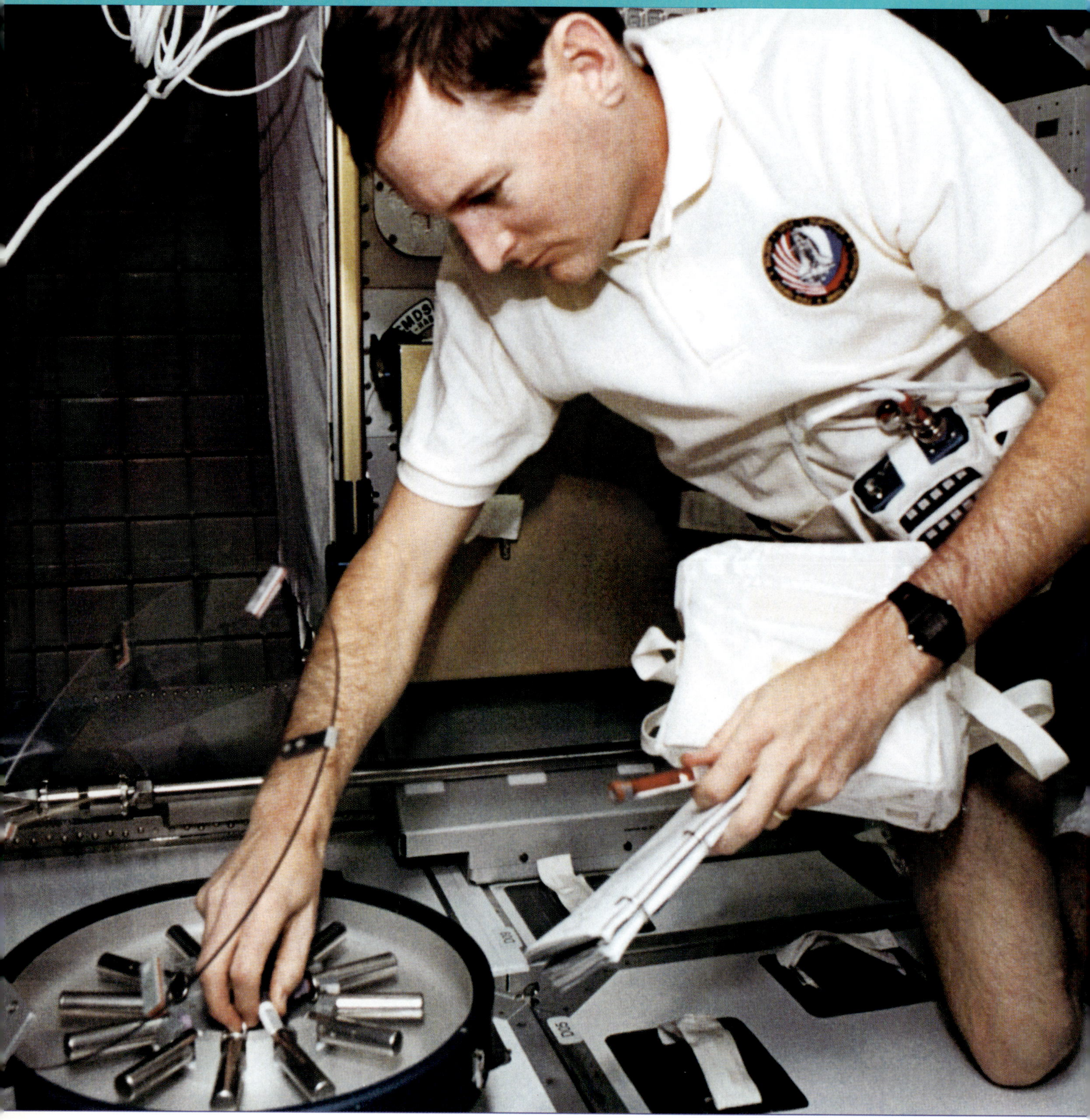

The spacecraft are built at different factories.

CLINK! CLANK!

Then they come back to the center to be checked.

Engineers check everything. They are very careful people.

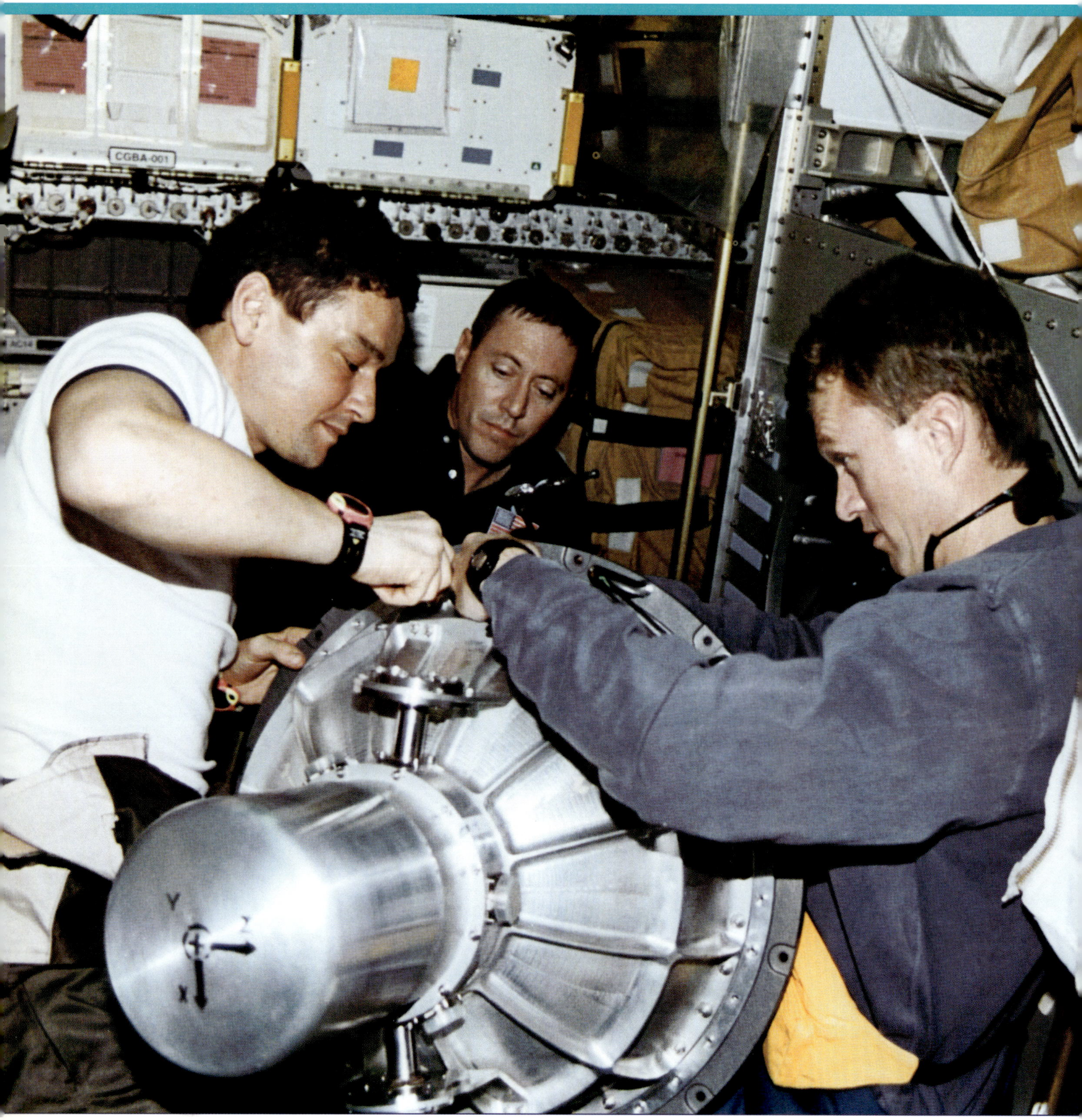
CGBA-001
Y
Z
X

Engineers run many tests on the spacecraft.

THUMP! CLICK! BOING!

They make sure the spacecraft will work in space.

Many things are different in space.

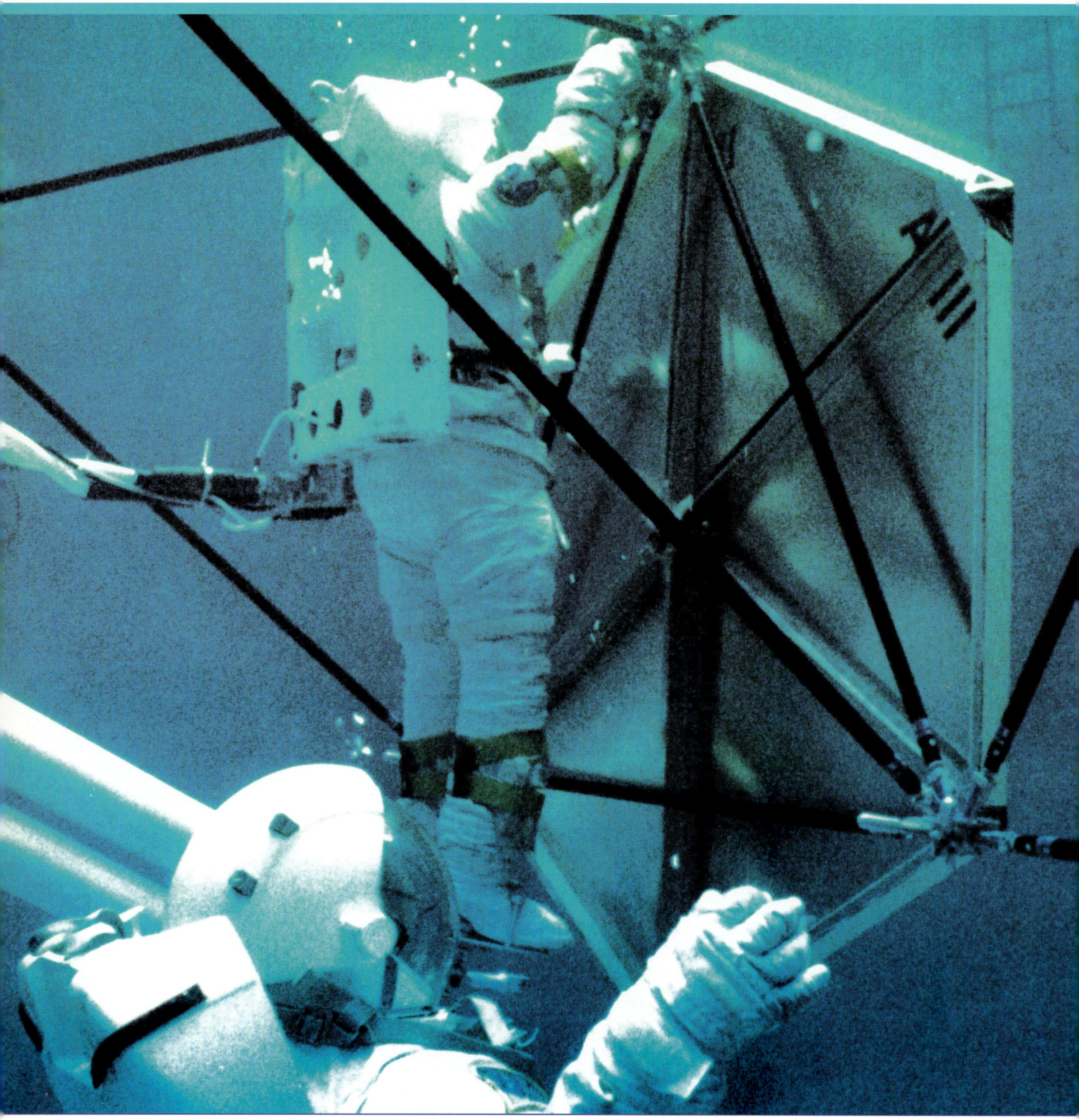

Let's go to Huntington Beach, California, now.
NASA people work here, too.
GLUB! BLUB!
It is a good place to do underwater tests.

So this is Huntington Beach!

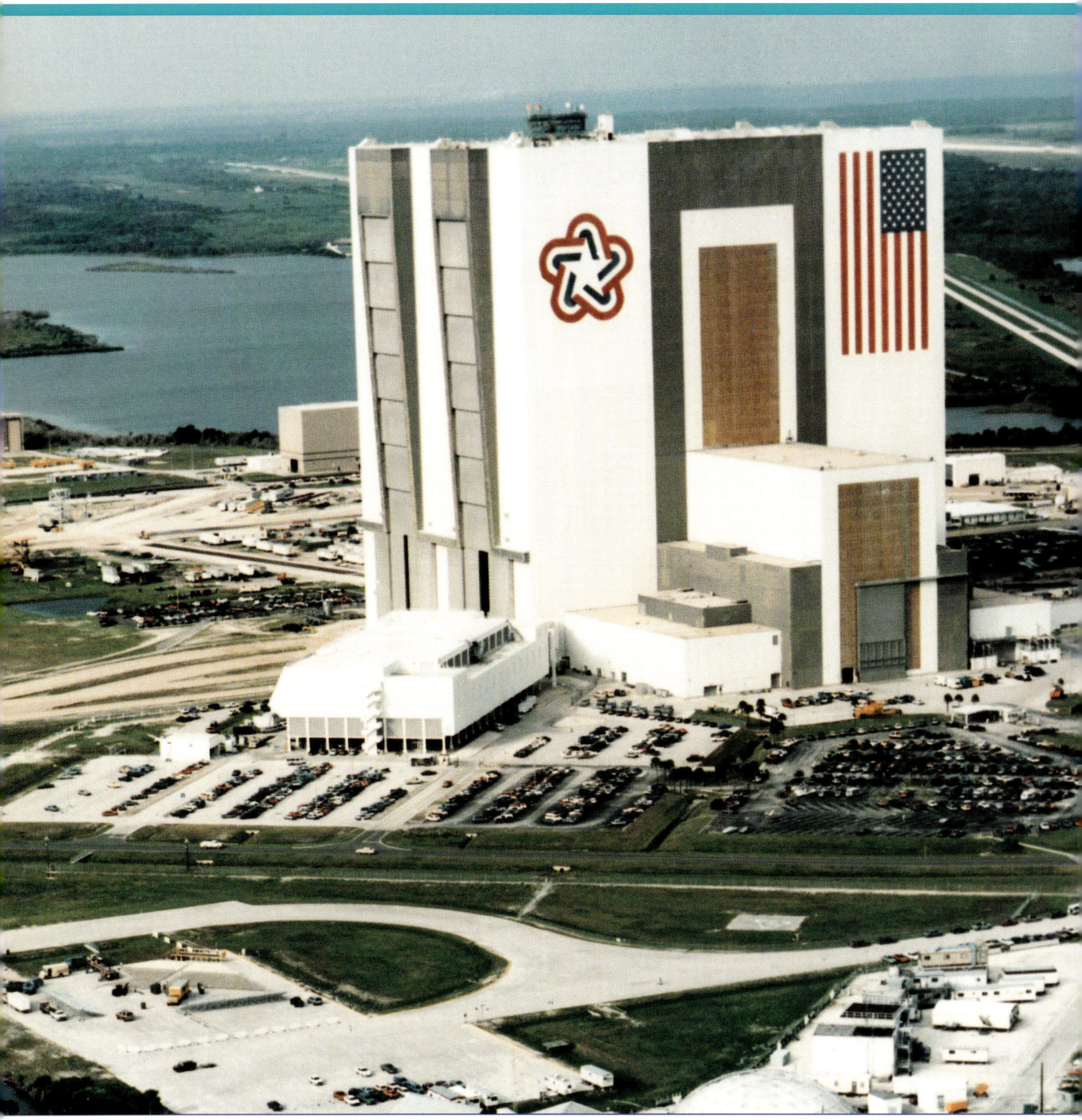

ZOOM! ZOOM!

We've traveled all across the country
to the John F. Kennedy Space Center in Florida.
This is where NASA launches the space shuttles.
And most of them land here after their flights.

Here we are on Merritt Island. It is near Cape Canaveral, Florida.

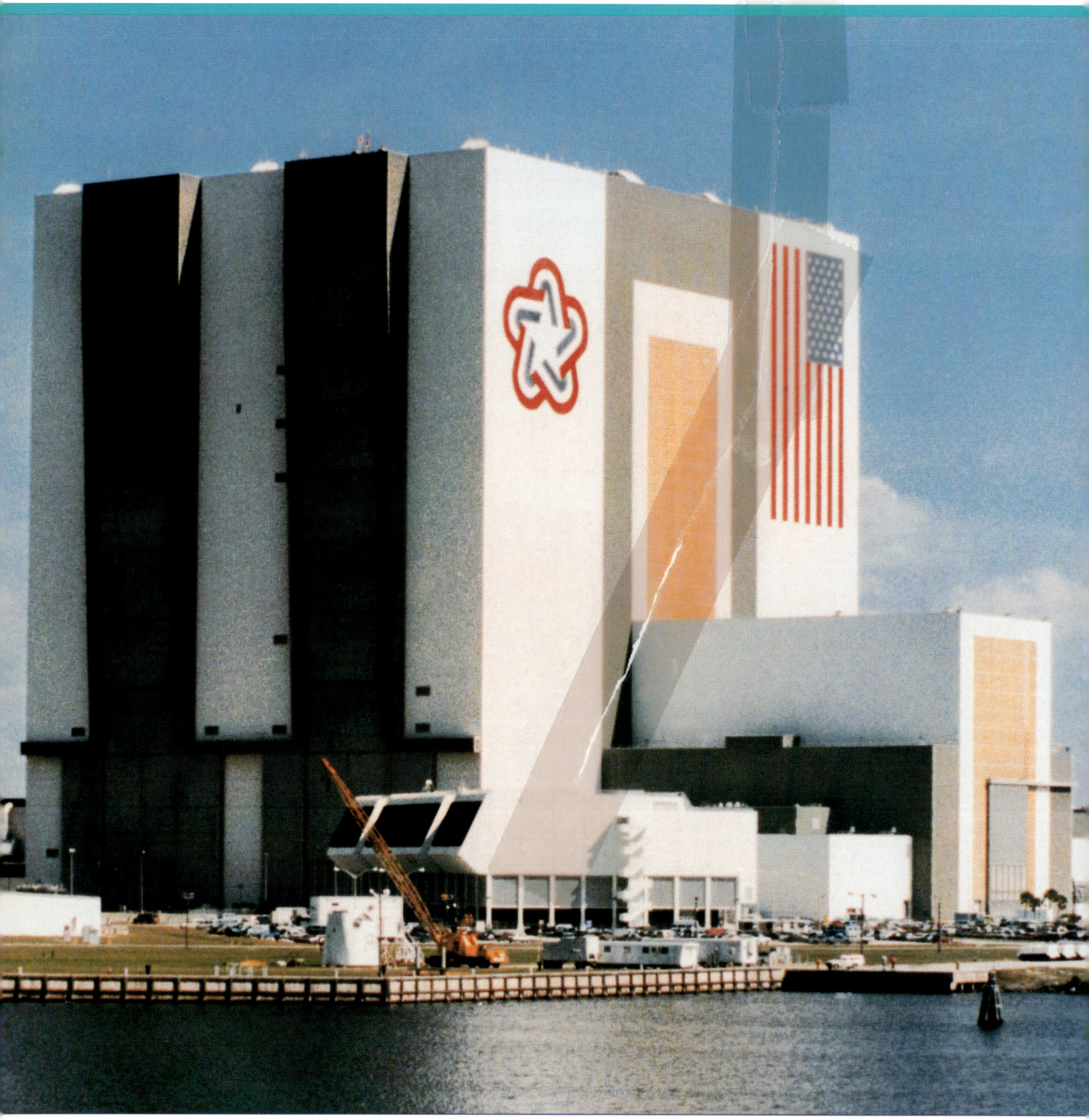

The Vehicle Assembly Building is five stories tall. This is where workers get the space shuttle ready for launch.

I hope that building has elevators!

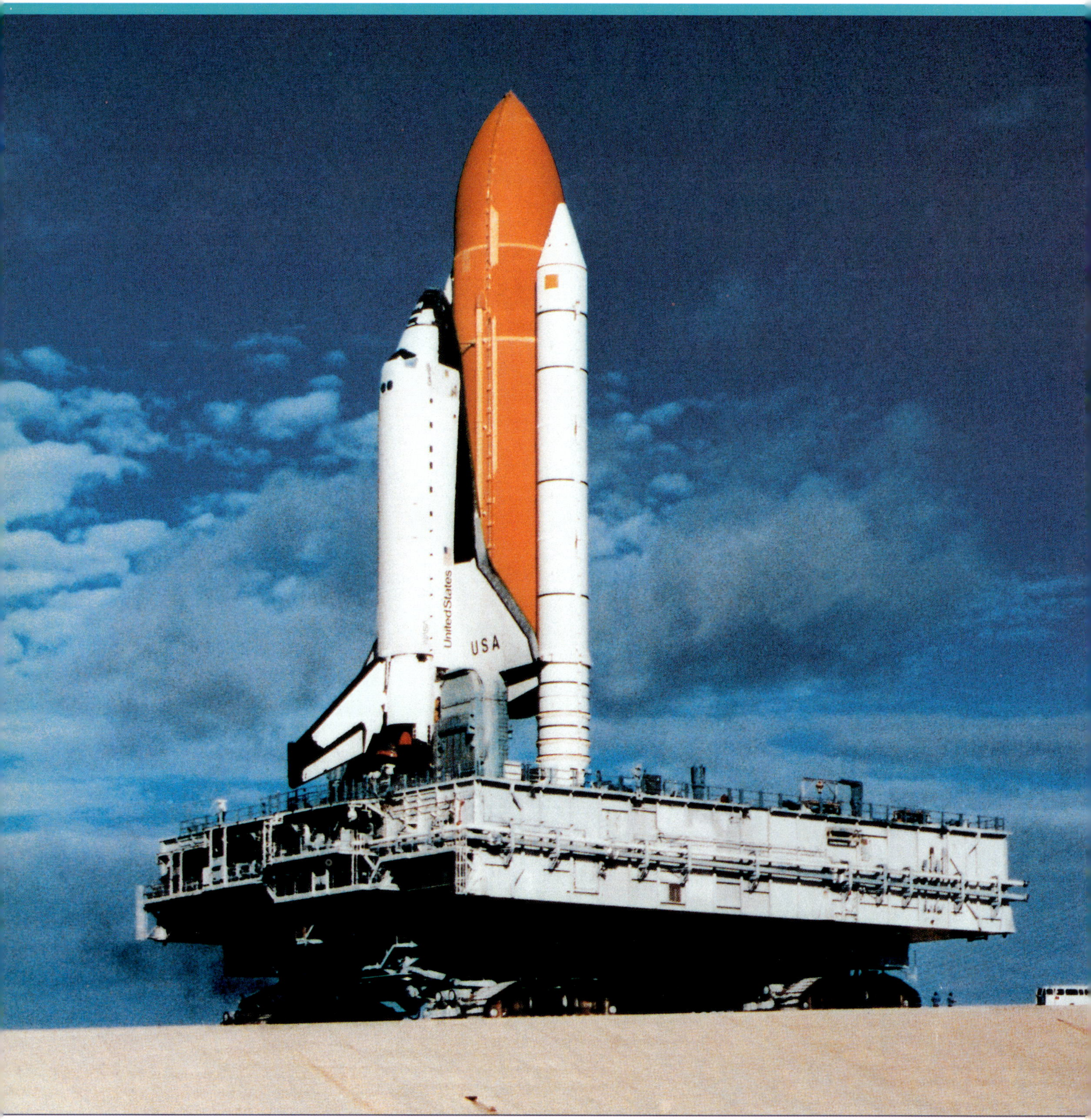
United States
USA

CHUG! CHUG! CHUG!

A huge machine called a crawler takes the space shuttle to a launch pad. The trip is about 3 ½ miles. It takes about 5 ½ hours.

No wonder that machine is called a crawler!

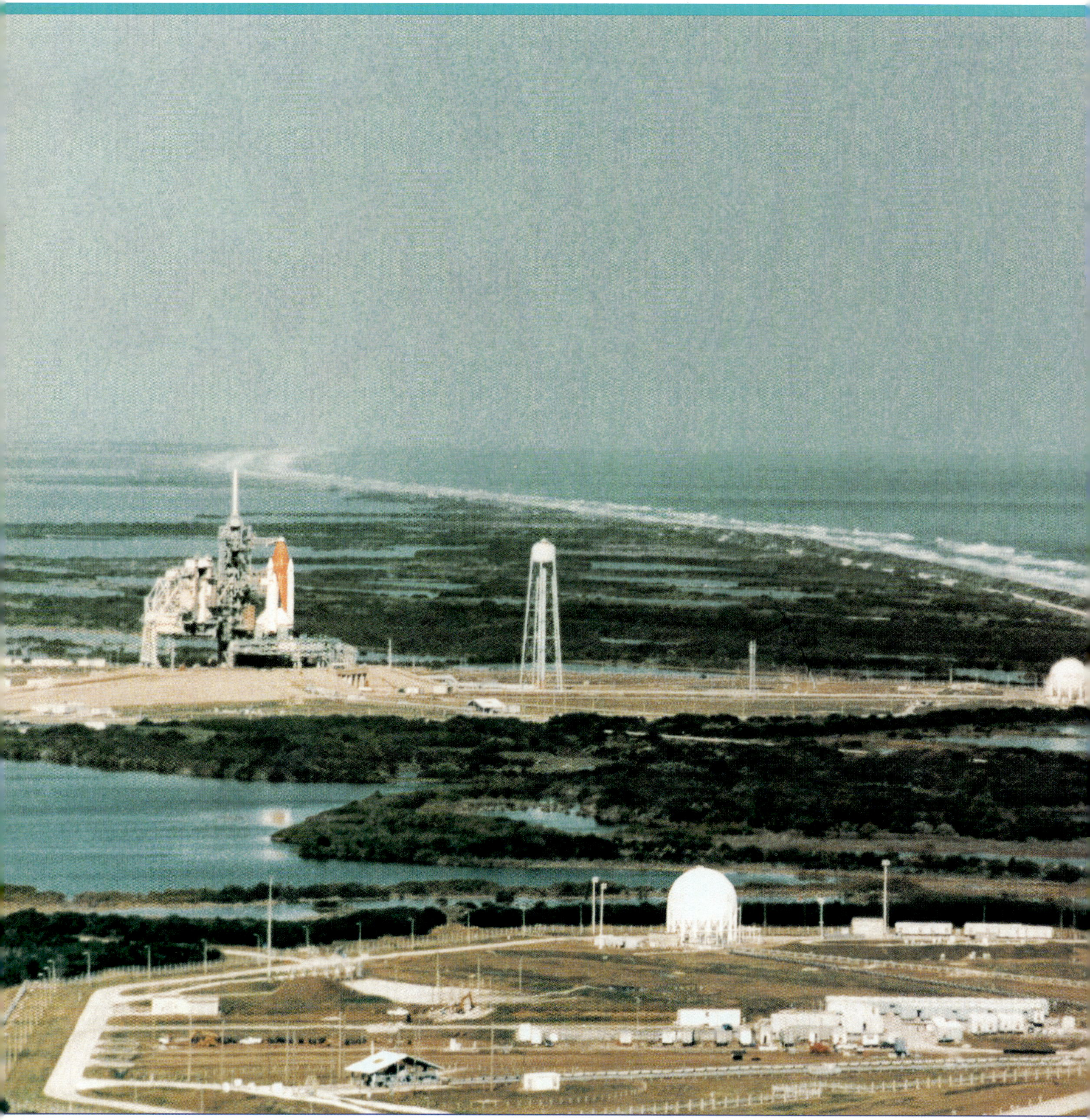

The Kennedy Space Center has two launch pads—A and B. This space shuttle is at Pad B.

I'll bet the astronauts are getting excited by now.

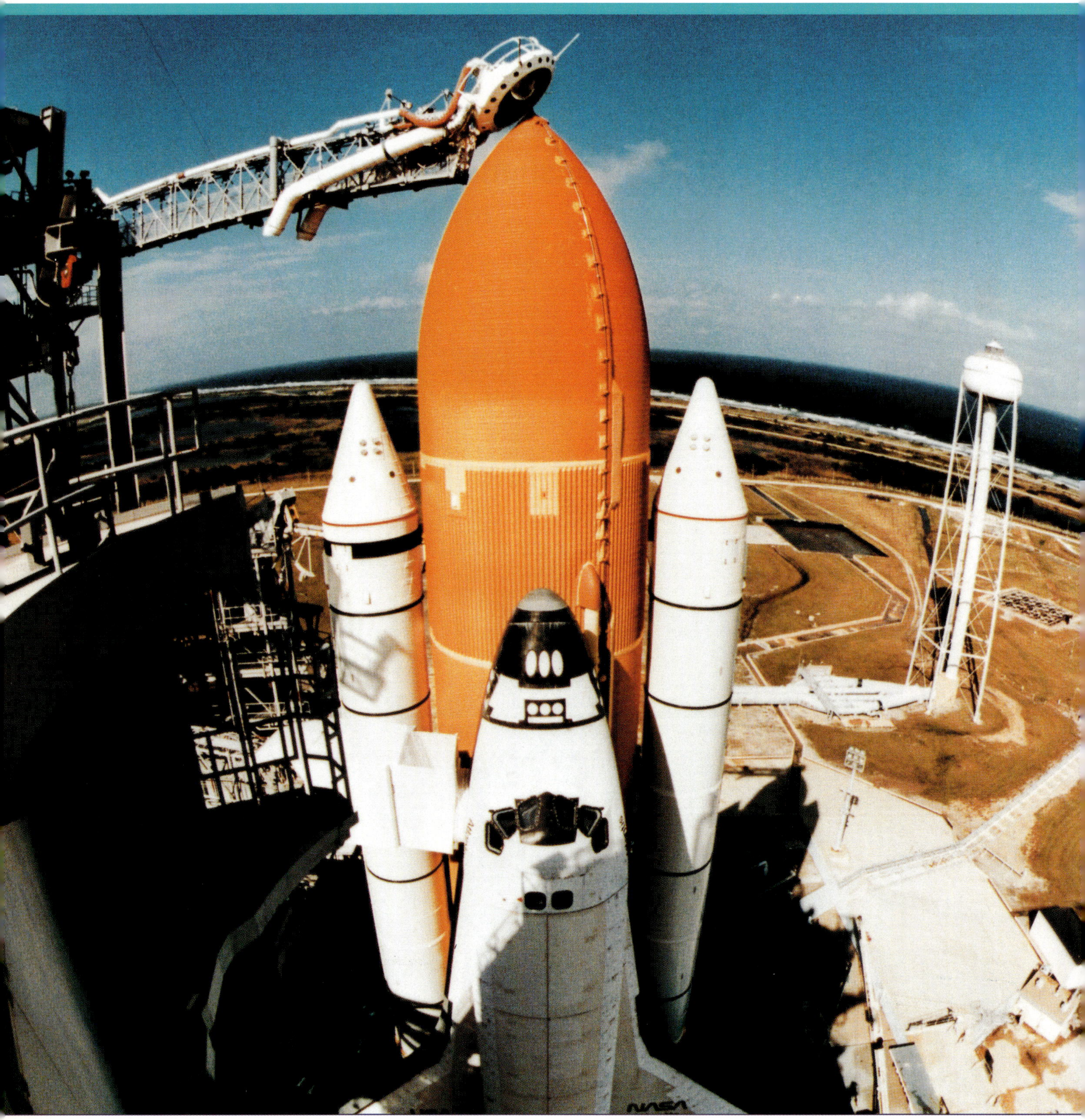
NASA

CREAK! CREAK! RATTLE!
Now the service structure is rolled away from the shuttle. Everything is almost ready. If all goes well, the space shuttle will be launched in about 11 hours.

But sometimes bad weather stops a launching. And sometimes the machinery is not working properly.

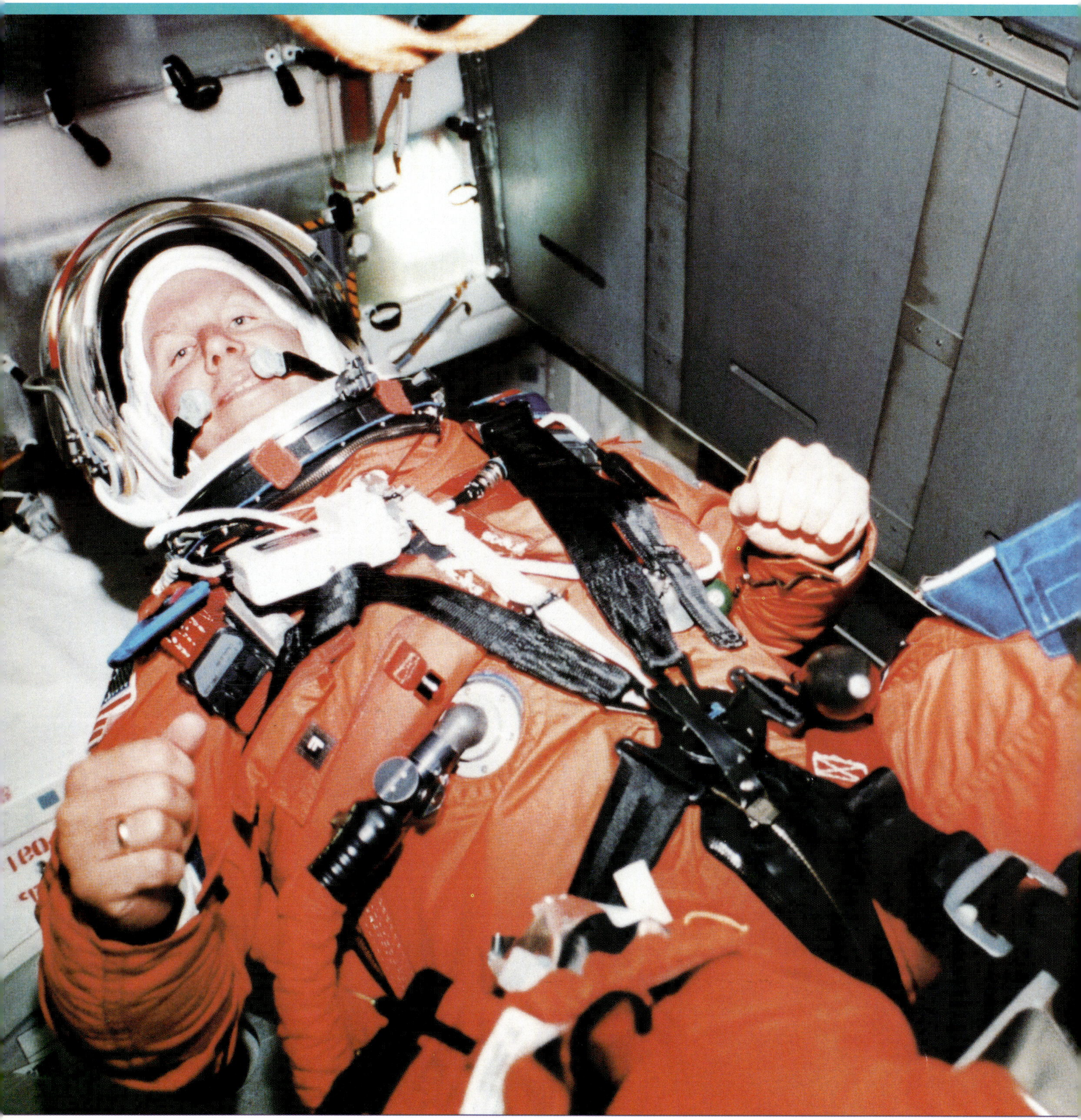

Before the real launching, the astronauts hold a dress rehearsal. They know that everything must be perfect. Every last thing!
This astronaut is on the middeck.

The middeck doesn't look very comfortable.

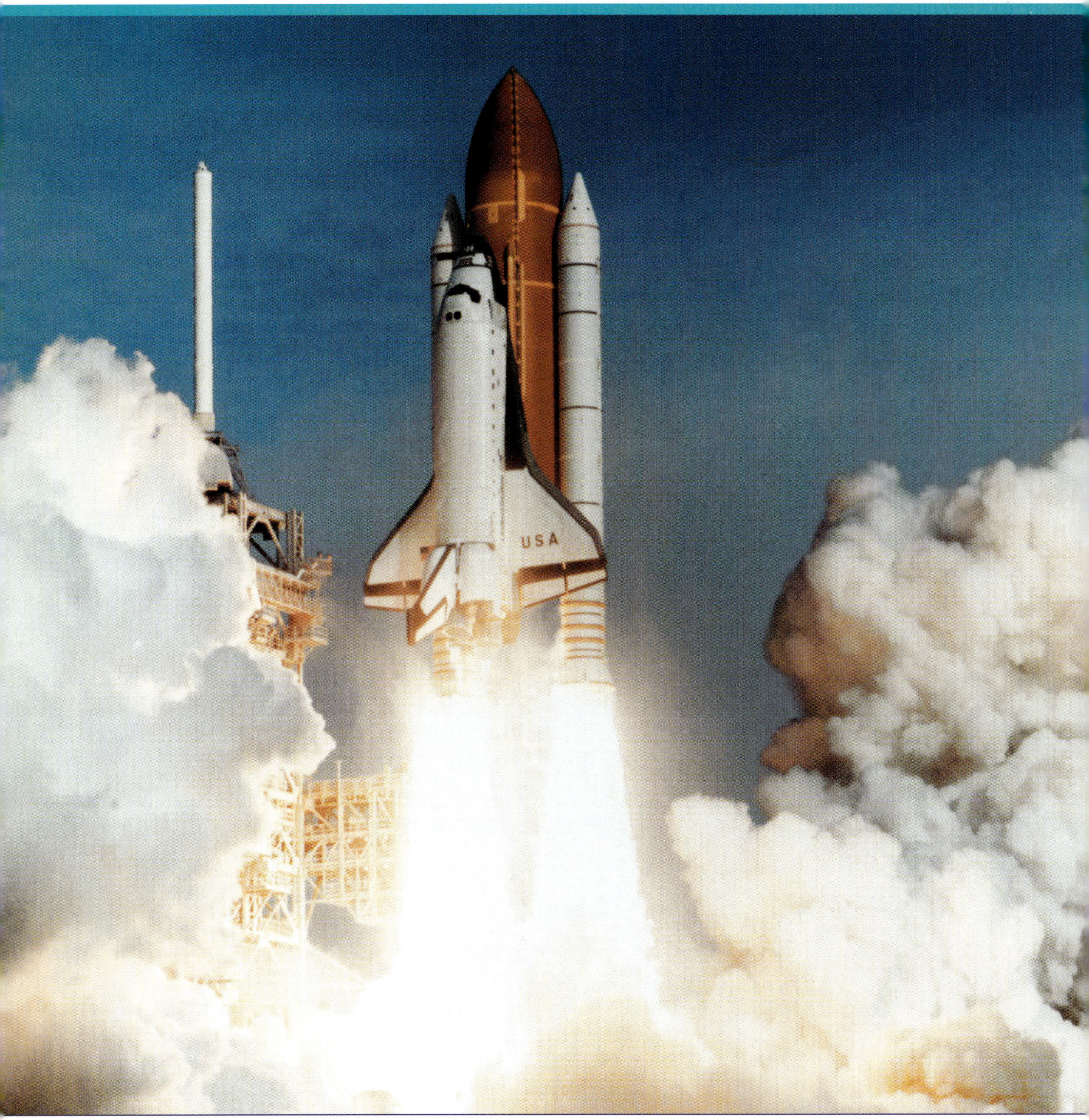
USA

Everyone at all the space centers
is holding their breath.
The countdown begins.
And it's LIFTOFF!

Isn't that beautiful!

Glossary

astronaut — person trained to work in space

computer — a special machine that can hold information and give answers quickly

controls — a set of instruments used to start, steer, and stop a machine

flight — the motion of an object, usually an airplane, through the air

lift-off — take-off

NASA — The National Aeronautics and Space Administration — the part of the government that is in charge of the space program for the United States of America

problems — difficulties; troubles

shuttle — the craft built to allow astronauts to fly into space and return to Earth

space — the huge place where the planets, sun, stars, and other heavenly objects are found

spacecraft — a vehicle built to travel in space safely

About the Author
Carol Greene has written over 200 books for children. She also likes to read books, make teddy bears, work in her garden, and sing songs.
Ms. Greene lives in Webster Groves, Missouri.